Find Your AWESOME

A 30-DAY CHALLENGE TO FALL IN LOVE WITH YOUR PLAYFUL, IMAGINATIVE & COLORFUL SELF

A CREATIVE JOURNAL ADVENTURE

Judy Clement Wall

Health Communications, Inc.
Deerfield Beach, Florida

www.hcibooks.com

Library of Congress Cataloging-in-Publication Data
is available through the Library of Congress

ISBN-13: 978-07573-1975-4 (Paperback)
ISBN-10: 07573-1975-0 (Paperback)
ISBN-13: 978-07573-1976-1 (ePub)
ISBN-10: 07573-1976-9 (ePub)

Publisher: Health Communications, Inc.
       3201 S.W. 15th Street
       Deerfield Beach, FL 33442–8190

Illustrations by © Judy Clement Wall
Cover design by Andrea Perrine Brower
Inside layout by Lawna Patterson Oldfield

THIS
JOURNAL
BELONGS TO

_____

HELLO!

I'm so excited you're here with this journal committing yourself to 30 days of self-love and exploration. In a perfect world, maybe you wouldn't need a 30-day challenge to find and fall in love with your most playful, imaginative, and colorful self, but we don't live in a perfect world. We live in a fast-paced, info-packed, high-octane society where feeling lost in the jostling crowd is the norm and locating our own significance is sometimes the biggest challenge of all.

jostling crowd

you

During a particularly difficult time in my life, when I was struggling both professionally and personally, I used my blog to publicly commit myself to a Year of Fearless Love. I went into that year needing to believe in the power we all have to touch, lift, and heal each other. My goal (though I don't know if I could have articulated it at the time) was to prove that hypothesis true.

Every month I gave myself a challenge. I hugged strangers; performed acts of mushy, unabashed gratitude; and left anonymous notes of encouragement in unexpected places. I blogged about my activities, and over the course of the year, others joined me. By the end of my experiment, there were people loving more fearlessly all over the world. In Connecticut, a woman with cancer texted love relentlessly, until she broke through her own feelings of resentment and anger. In Canada, a woman began her own project: a Year of Hugging Fearlessly. She hugged people all over the globe and posted photos of each embrace. In Portland, a woman decided to take a chance on love. She's married now. In Romania, a woman blogged right along with me. She did every challenge I did and wrote about each one. She reminded me of how far love can reach.

I learned so much during that time, but the thing that surprised me most was how much easier it was for people to turn their love outward. They had no trouble writing love letters and performing random acts of kindness…until the moment I asked them to redirect that loving attention to themselves.

It broke my heart to see how people struggled to show themselves the same sort of sweetness and patience they so willingly showed to others. For a whole host of reasons, all of them seemingly justified, we put ourselves last day after day. We spend so much time being there for our friends and our families, our colleagues and our neighbors, that there is precious little time left over for taking care of ourselves.

It's hard to break that habit of unhealthy selflessness, in part because our society encourages it. Tell people how busy you are, how much work you have to do, how many deadlines are looming, and they will smile sympathetically. They know your pain. By contrast, it's uncomfortable to talk about self love. Tell people you're maneuvering your own personal, breathtaking evolution and they will look at you like you just announced you're marrying a hamster.

But here's what I know for sure: At the center of every truly important and meaningful thing we do, there is love. It connects us to each other and to our planet. It fuels our best work and our bravest art. In the final moments of our lives, how well we loved will be the measure of how well we lived. And all love begins with self-love.

It is a miraculous and wonderful truth that when you learn to love and value yourself, your relationships with everyone else change, because the *you* that you bring into those relationships is the fullest, truest, best-loved version of yourself.

So this journal is about filling your well. It's about inviting yourself to play, and in the process, discovering once and for all the undeniable awesomeness that is you.

The Rules

There are no rules.

This journal absolutely, positively *doesn't* have to be completed in 30 days. In fact, almost all of these activities can easily be stretched beyond one day, into their own 30-day challenges, or (better yet!) into lifelong practices.

The point here is to love yourself with all the heart, creativity, and good humor you can muster. If it takes you more than 30 days, all the better!

Life is short. Live accordingly.
~ Patti Digh

30 Days of Self-Love

- [x] Day 1: Text Love ♥
- [x] Day 2: Celebrate Your Body
- [x] Day 3: Make a Rockin'-Your-Life List
- [ ] Day 4: Put Yourself on a T-Shirt
- [ ] Day 5: Be Outrageously Grateful
- [ ] Day 6: Make a Mandala
- [ ] Day 7: Call Bullshit on *Should*
- [ ] Day 8: Be Openly Magnificent
- [ ] Day 9: Fill in the Spaces
- [ ] Day 10: Be Wildly Creative
- [ ] Day 11: Hold a Burning Ceremony
- [ ] Day 12: Doodle Your Loves
- [ ] Day 13: Hug It Out
- [ ] Day 14: List 10 People You're Grateful For
- [ ] Day 15: Organize Something

Woo hoo! You're halfway done!

- ☐ Day 16: Unplug
- ☐ Day 17: Make a Songs-to-Belt List
- ☐ Day 18: Be Unapologetic
- ☐ Day 19: Write a Self-Love Mantra
- ☐ Day 20: Write Your Personal Manifesto
- ☐ Day 21: Leave It Here
- ☐ Day 22: Leave Love Lying Around
- ☐ Day 23: Practice Pleasure
- ☐ Day 24: Make a *Not*-to-Do List
- ☐ Day 25: Decide What Matters
- ☐ Day 26: Take a Break
- ☐ Day 27: Be Surprising
- ☐ Day 28: Draw a Self-Portrait
- ☐ Day 29: Write Yourself a Love Letter
- ☐ Day 30: Design a Book Cover for Your Life Story

Stand Tall!
You're a Self-Love Warrior!

❐ DAY 1: TEXT LOVE

In December of 2010, I got a text message from a friend. It said, "Hey J, you're beautiful"—that's it. Just four words, but they changed first the course of my day . . . and then, my life.

Honestly, the impact of that message amazed me, even at the time. It lifted me from the foul mood I was in before it came, and it got me thinking (obsessively, over days and then weeks) about the power of kindness, the ease with which we truly can bring more love into the world. It stirred my imagination, inspiring me to spend the next year of my life devoted to all that can be discovered and accomplished at the intersection of fearlessness and love.

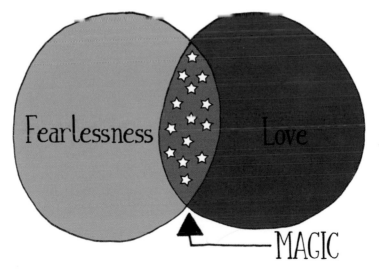

Fearlessness

Love

MAGIC

Even writing it now, I find the story fantastical. How does a simple text from a friend have such an outsized impact on a life? But it happened to me, so I know it's true. I know, with absolute certainty, the ripple effect of our actions, that crazy-wonderful tendency of love to spread to the edges of things, and beyond.

And the best part about acting on your most loving impulses? It turns out that kind gestures, whether you're on the giving or the receiving end, make you happier. It has to do with dopamine and the reward centers of your brain, but for our purposes, let's just say that if we're all connected, then what I do for you, I do for me, and vice versa.

Don't believe me? Try it! This is the first day of your self-love adventure; spend it sending love texts. Be sweet. Be surprising. Be a goofball. Do it generously, without strings, without expectation. Text your lover, your friends, your mom, your kid. Say "I love you," as only you can.

One of my most wonderfully weird friends texted me this out of nowhere: "If you told me you were going to dye your hair, I'd beg you not to." Maybe you have to know him to get how sweet that was, but it totally melted me. My point is, there are lots of ways to say I love you. Have fun with this challenge and let the dopamine flow!

(Note: Texting love is an excellent habit to adopt. Three out of four doctors recommend texting love daily for a healthier heart ... yet I have serious doubts about whether that fourth guy is even a real doctor.)

❒ DAY 2: CELEBRATE YOUR BODY

Too many of us spend an inordinate amount of time lamenting our bodies. We're too fat, too skinny, too tall, too short. We're too old, stiff, tired, wrinkled. Our butts are big; our chests are small. We're not strong, or fast, or graceful enough. We look at Photoshopped models and wish we were perfect, even as we rail against our society's preoccupation with an aesthetic that has nothing to do with real, soulful beauty.

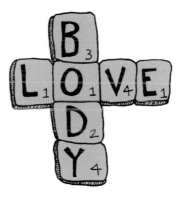

Today, be grateful for your body, for all the stuff it does, and for the way it so masterfully holds all your insides in place. (Imagine if it didn't!) Celebrate your curves and your hard-earned scars, your miraculous central nervous system, and your dependable eyelids. Love your shoulders, your wrists, your ankles, and elbows. Appreciate the steps your feet take, the leaps they're capable of. Marvel at your astonishing, opposable thumbs!

Start a habit today of complimenting your body. It deserves all the love you can dish out.

DEAR ARMS:
THANK YOU FOR HUGGING.
HUGGING IS GOOD!

ELBOWS, I LOVE
YOUR BENDY WAYS!

YOU'RE BEAUTIFUL,
SMILE!

THANKS FOR HAVING
MY BACK, SPINE!

BELLY, NO ONE LAUGHS
BETTER THAN YOU!

BUTT, WHAT CAN I SAY?
YOU ARE ALWAYS THERE
FOR ME. THANK YOU!

HEY, LEGS, THANK YOU FOR
DANCING. I PROMISE WE'LL
DO MORE OF THAT.

Okay, it's your turn. Fill in the blanks with some outrageous body love!

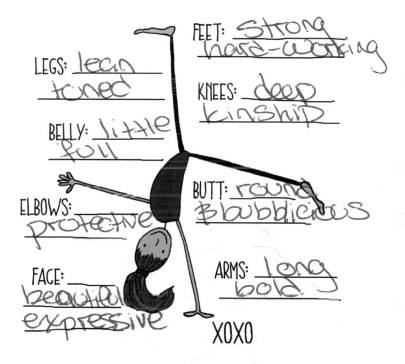

LEGS: lean toned

BELLY: little full

ELBOWS: protective

FACE: beautiful expressive

FEET: strong hard-working

KNEES: deep kinship

BUTT: round Bbubblicious

ARMS: long bold

XOXO

❒ DAY 3: MAKE A ROCKIN'-YOUR-LIFE LIST

Do you already have a list of things you want to do before you die? If so, yay! If not, it's time to make one, and here's why.

First, it's fun to create a list of big, small, realistic, pie-in-the-sky, ordinary, extraordinary, before-you-die goals. It encourages you to imagine both the sweeping landscape and the intricate details of the life you most want to live.

Second, something superhero-y happens, I believe, when you marry your goal-setting self to your whimsical, dreamy self. Maps get made, plans get drawn up, northbound steps get taken.

Third, lists make things feel possible. It's something about their specificity, their unassailable, enumerated logic. If you can list it, you can accomplish it.

So that's today's goal. Make a list of the big and little things you want to do before you leave this planet. Or, if you already have a Rockin'-Your-Life list, pick an item on it, and today take the first step toward making it happen. Write the first paragraph of your book, buy some language tapes, sign up for a class, get your passport … whatever stirs your imagination right now.

Here's my doodley list …

MY ROCKIN'-MY-LIFE LIST

1. GO ON A SAFARI
2. WRITE A BOOK 3. PUBLISH A BOOK
4. BE A CAMPAIGN VOLUNTEER
5. EXPLORE ZION NATIONAL PARK
6. GO ON A TRAIN TRIP

7. PRACTICE YOGA 8. GO ON A YOGA RETREAT
9. START A MOVEMENT 10. MEET A HERO
11. TAKE A ROAD TRIP
12. RIDE A GONDOLA
13. LEARN A NEW LANGUAGE
14. LIVE ABROAD
15. CREATE MY OWN FONT
16. DESIGN A (COMMISSIONED) POSTER
17. PAINT A MURAL
18. ANIMATE SOMETHING
19. MAKE A METAL SOMETHING
20. LEARN TO KNIT

We get everywhere we want to go in life the same way: one self-loving step at a time.

So, now it's your turn: make a list!

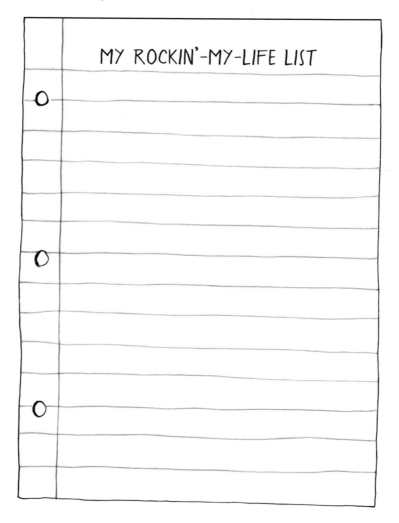

MY ROCKIN'-MY-LIFE LIST

❑ DAY 4: PUT YOURSELF ON A T-SHIRT

T-shirts are kind of like tattoos in that they are a wearable art form that says something true about you. It's an imperfect comparison, I know. T-shirts, unlike tattoos, aren't permanent, so most of us don't think as hard about the messages they give to the world. The T-shirt I'm wearing right now, for instance, says only that I'm behind on laundry. My badass-hippie-love-warrior T-shirt is a better example because I think it says everything important to know about me.

Fact:
there can never be
too many
BADASS
open-hearted
hippie
warriors
of **LOVE**.

What would your perfect T-shirt say about you right now? Mine would say this:

Or maybe this:

Okay, now it's your turn. Color, doodle, craft a T-shirt (or two, or three) to tell the world some truths about you.

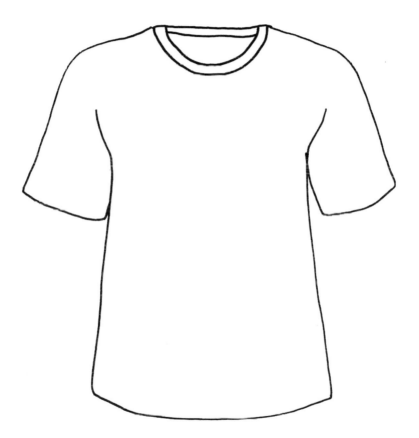

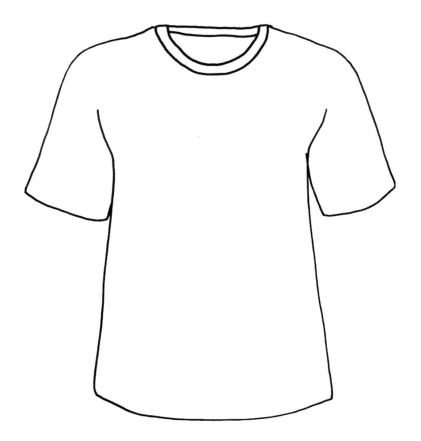

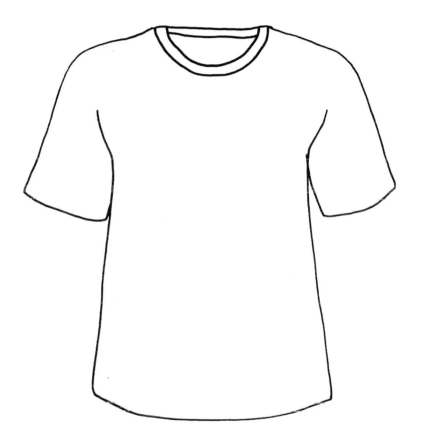

❐ DAY 5: BE OUTRAGEOUSLY GRATEFUL

One of the hardest things to overcome when practicing self-love is the feeling that we don't deserve our own esteem. After all, we know ourselves better than anyone. We know how judgmental we can be. We know when we're being lazy or procrastinating, and we know all the excuses we make for not showing up.

We are, for better *and* worse, intimately familiar with our flaws, and that knowledge can make us feel lesser. Over time, we can become convinced that we're not (successful, smart, beautiful, popular, educated, affluent, daring, thin, savvy, articulate, enlightened, brave) enough.

We start to suspect we have nothing of value to offer. That isn't true, of course. We hold ourselves to an impossible standard of perfection and then feel inadequate when we don't measure up. We're ridiculously hard on ourselves, but I've discovered an antidote to that terrible (and false) feeling of lack, and it's gratitude-big, mushy, unabashed gratitude. Surprised? Let me explain.

I'm not talking about a gratitude journal, or a jar, or a meditative ritual. Those are great, too, but what I'm talking about is more communal. I'm talking about engaging in concrete, outward, unmistakable acts of heartfelt appreciation.

I'm talking about writing something nice with the tip you leave in a restaurant. Telling someone's manager what a great job they did for you. Writing thank-you notes and sending ardent, immediate gratitude texts. E-mailing a favorite author, artist, teacher, or activist to say how much you appreciate their work. Calling someone to say, "The world is better with you in it." Treating someone to coffee. Giving your conscious, focused, undivided attention without reservation because someone you love deserves it.

Spend today committing random acts of thankfulness, and you'll find it's impossible to stay in that "not enough" place. By necessity, physical acts of gratitude focus your mind and body on what you have, rather than on what you lack, and the effects of that focus last far longer than the time it takes to send someone a card or take a friend out to lunch.

So, that's your goal today. Be outrageously grateful. Notice all the good things in your life, from the existence of pizza, to the magic of gravity, to all the (equally imperfect and beautiful) beings who love you just the way you are.

And then come back here and fill the next couple of pages with the story of your outrageous gratitude.

☐ DAY 6: MAKE A MANDALA

Here's the truth that I want you to focus on today: you are complete all by yourself, just as you are.

You don't need anyone's validation or approval. There is no job or career, no degree or award, no zip code or bank balance that will make you more worthy than you are right now, this minute. Because right now, this minute, you are priceless—absolutely unique in a world chock full of humans.

Are you wondering what that fact has to do with making a mandala?

Well, while it's true that originally mandalas were religious and spiritual symbols meant to repre-sent the universe, these days, they are used more widely. They've gone mainstream; their circular shape and geometric patterns are often used in art and meditation to impart a sense of beauty, wholeness, and order. And that's what we're after today.

I speak from experience when I say that drawing a mandala is not only a creative adventure, but a meditative and restorative one as well. It allows you to get quiet and focused, to let go of your self-doubt and inner critic, and lose yourself in the process of creation. The repetition that is inherent to drawing patterns can be soothing in the same way as a mantra repeated during meditation, or the rhythmic sound of waves lapping a shore.

So today, we're making a mandala. You can finish one I started, draw one yourself, or color one I drew for you. Or you can do all three, as the mandala-making super nova you never knew you were!

No matter what you do, remember this as you play:

You are whole. You are complete. You are, to quote Rumi, the universe in ecstatic motion.

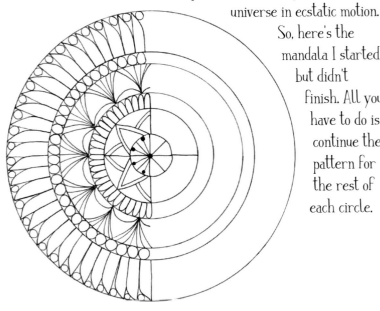

So, here's the mandala I started but didn't finish. All you have to do is continue the pattern for the rest of each circle.

And here's the one I did finish. It just needs some color.

Ready to tackle your own?

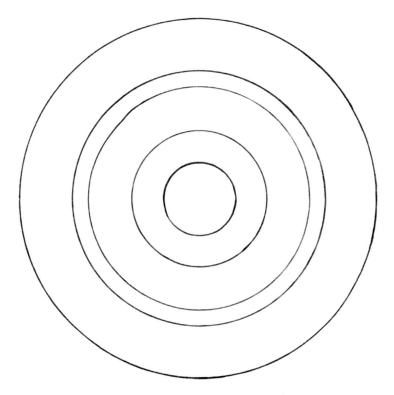

❐ DAY 7: CALL BULLSHIT ON *SHOULD*

There are two kinds of should-things. There are the things you do because you should, and there are the things you *don't* do, but think you should. The first kind makes you feel heavy and unenthused about life, and the second makes you feel guilty and inadequate.

Both suck, so today, I don't want you to do anything for which the only justification is "I should."

I know what you're thinking. *What about going to work? What about cleaning my office, working out, calling my mom, paying my bills?*

I see your point. There are some obligations that you can't shirk. But that's okay, because it's not necessarily the tasks themselves I want to get rid of, it's the "I should" thoughts around them.

You've heard it a hundred times, I know, but it's true. What you focus on expands. If you're focused on the dread of doing this thing you don't want to do, it affects everything in your life-your perception of the world, your energy level, your feelings about yourself, and even the way others perceive you. Negative energy is a powerful thing.

But sometimes it really is as simple as reframing the task at hand. If today you're determined to do nothing out of obligation or guilt, then you'll clean your office because decluttering makes room for creativity. You'll meet yourself on the yoga mat because balance is exhilarating. You'll call your mom because you can—because she's still here on this planet, and so are you, and how wonderful is that?

It sounds crazy, but try it. Reframe anything on your to-do list that feels like an obligation. And if you can't reframe it, if you can't find the golden truth that makes it worth doing, then call bullshit on it. Don't do it, and don't feel bad about your choice.

Here's how that works: don't meditate, because you don't like to. Don't vacuum because, in the interest of science, you've decided to build up your tolerance to dust. Don't organize your closet because there's a good book and a sweet cat on the couch, both in dire need of your attention.

Just for today, call bullshit on "should," reframe your world, and see what happens.

❏ DAY 8: BE OPENLY MAGNIFICENT

Instead of trying to fit in, instead of making yourself small so that others feel big, instead of being quiet and polite and perfectly acceptable, be openly magnificent today.

Shine. Laugh loud and belly-deep. Be the center of attention. Flaunt your intelligence, your humor, your absolute grasp of the situation. Strut. Take up space-meaningfully, beautifully, unapologetically. Move to your own music. Sway. Shimmy. Twirl. Own your opinions, your mistakes, and your triumphs. Be fearlessly and unabashedly *you*.

Today, live your life like you mean it. Then tomorrow, do it again. And the next day, and the next day, and the next day . . .

And while you're at it, use the next page to make a list of your superpowers-the things that others look to you for because they come naturally to you, like listening without judgment or connecting the right people to each other.

◻ DAY 9: FILL IN THE SPACES

Fill these spaces with doodles, with color, with lines or circles, poetry, or rants. Dive deep, be silly, or use these pages to commit random acts of beauty. There is so much in our lives that we can't control, today you can turn these little spaces into whatever you need them to be.

Here are some spaces I filled . . .

Okay, your turn, have fun!

⌐ DAY 10: BE WILDLY CREATIVE

Because it is a form of self-expression, I believe that every act of creation is also an act of self-love. I can't think of anything more basic and beautiful than our human desire to create, to make something out of nothing, or change something old into something new.

Engaging creatively is like a full-body workout for the soul. In doing so, we honor our time, our instincts, our tender (often unspoken) ideas, and we connect with the most adventurous, evolutionary part of ourselves.

So make something today! Have fun with it, and in case you need some inspiration, I made a list of suggestions (enough to stretch Day 10 into its own 30-day challenge!)

THINGS TO MAKE

1. Music
2. A dream catcher
3. A "this is me" collage
4. A finger painting
5. Art made from discarded things
6. A new friend
7. A handmade card
8. Something with duct tape
9. An epic doodle
10. Cupcakes
11. A difference
12. A city made of playing cards
13. A pizza
14. A beautiful mess
15. Someone's day
16. A papier-mâché sculpture
17. A brand-new cocktail named after yourself
18. A bouquet of paper flowers
19. A date with someone you love

THINGS TO MAKE LIST (cont.)

20. A date with yourself
21. A peace-love-hope yard sign
22. Something with yarn
23. A new dance move
24. A paper snowflake
25. An entrance
26. Some chalky sidewalk art
27. A "find your happy" playlist
28. A list of small pleasures
29. Something with Popsicle sticks
30. Love

DAY 11: HOLD A BURNING CEREMONY

I believe that the secret to loving yourself more and better lies in letting go. There is such freedom in shedding your limiting beliefs, the stories that no longer feel like yours, and the wounds that never quite heal. Letting go is an act of supreme generosity to your soul. On my own self-love journey, I've let go of so many outdated and ill-fitting stories, and one of my favorite ways to do that is with a burning ceremony.

There's something about the ritual that imbues your intention to let go with a reassuring, tangible weight. It creates an actual moment of release, a "before-you," and an "after-you." When I have done this in the past, the "after-me" always feels lighter, more conscious, loving, and hopeful.

BEFORE-ME

AFTER-ME

There is no right or wrong way to hold a burning ceremony, but this is how I do it.

First, I write something I want to let go of down on a piece of paper. Usually, it's a thorny, recurring hurt or frustration, something I've wrestled with, written about, cried over, something I finally feel ready to release.

WHAT I'M LETTING
GO OF:

THE SHYNESS THAT
KEEPS ME FROM
SPEAKING UP.

An old story I used to tell myself...
but not anymore.

Once I've written it down, I fold the paper up and light a fire in the little pit in our backyard. Using tongs, I hold the paper over the flame until it catches, and then I watch it burn. I try to feel it inside me, the space that gets created as I watch this thing I've wrestled with literally turn to ashes and disappear.

Today, hold a burning ceremony. Create your own ritual, and let go of something big, because here's the truth: you are so much more than your old stories can tell. Now is the time to start shedding them and, in the moment of release, become the lighter, more fiercely self-loving and hopeful "after-you."

Use this page to draw or write out the feelings of before- and after-you!

BEFORE-YOU

AFTER-YOU

❏ DAY 12: DOODLE YOUR LOVES

What do you love? Pizza? Your pillow? Your pets? Your humans?
Paris? Summertime? Micron pens?

FILL THIS PAGE WITH DOODLES OF THE THINGS
YOU LOVE, BECAUSE THINKING ABOUT WHAT YOU
LOVE IS GOOD FOR THE SOUL.

❒ DAY 13: HUG IT OUT

During my Year of Fearless Love, I publicly committed to hugging someone new every day for 28 days. To meet the goal, I had to hug some people I didn't know, which is incredibly hard for an introvert like me.

I felt panicky asking strangers for hugs. Then, in a coffee shop one morning, I mustered up enough courage to explain my fearless love project to a couple I didn't know (Lindsay and Ben as it turns out, studying at a corner table). They both got up and hugged me. And so did Amanda, the barista. And then Kelly who was big, bald, goateed, and dressed in leather. And Ray, his friend, skinny, tattooed, fidgety, and a bit shy.

I remember noticing their expressions, as I did the expressions of everyone I hugged that February, how their faces went from surprise, to delight. I learned to love that expression, not just a smile, but a face breaking open, a mask-less, beautiful someone revealed.

I got addicted to being enfolded, addicted to the instant when I was standing heart-to-heart with a perfect stranger. I felt there was magic in that strange and sudden intimacy, devoid of barriers, baggage or bullshit . . . I felt precious then, believing each time that I'd entered a sacred space, that I would never be the same again.

Today, hug as many people as you can, as close as you can. Believe in the power of standing heart-to-heart. It is healing, as much for you as for everyone who enfolds you.

USE THIS PAGE TO MAKE A LIST OF PEOPLE
YOU'D LIKE TO HUG SOMEDAY. OPRAH? THE
DALAI LAMA? A BABY PANDA? (WHY LIMIT
YOURSELF TO ONLY PEOPLE, AFTER ALL!)

☐ DAY 14: LIST 10 PEOPLE YOU'RE GRATEFUL FOR

(... and then, if it feels right, tell them!)

1. ———————— BECAUSE————————
   ————————————————————

2. ———————— BECAUSE————————
   ————————————————————

3. ———————— BECAUSE————————
   ————————————————————

4. ———————— BECAUSE————————
   ————————————————————

5. ———————— BECAUSE————————
   ————————————————————

6. ———————— BECAUSE————————
   ————————————————————

7. ———————— BECAUSE————————
   ————————————————————

8. ———————— BECAUSE————————
   ————————————————————

9. ———————— BECAUSE————————
   ————————————————————

10. ———————— BECAUSE————————
    ————————————————————

❐ DAY 15: ORGANIZE SOMETHING

Getting organized feels good. Going through stuff, getting rid of what doesn't work or fit or suit you anymore, and then putting what's left in order. It's like shedding extra pounds or solving a mystery. And if you are one who thrives on clutter, have no fear: getting organized will clear the way for bigger, better messes!

So today, we're getting organized and here's how:

1. Pick a space; it can be as big as your garage or as small as your junk drawer. Sort everything in that space into piles.

   The first two piles—"recycle" and "throwaway"—are for anything broken.

THINGS TO BE RECYCLED OR THROWN AWAY

THE BLOW DRYER MY HUSBAND SAID TO "SAVE FOR PARTS."

PENS THAT DON'T WRITE. WHY DO I HAVE ALL THESE PENS THAT DON'T WRITE?

I HAVE AROUND A THOUSAND DEAD BATTERIES IN A BUCKET IN MY GARAGE. (I WISH I WERE KIDDING.)

The next pile is a "donate" pile for anything you haven't used in the last six months.

THINGS TO DONATE

MY CHRISTMAS UNICORN
SWEATER.... WHAT? →

COFFEE FILTERS
#4

← THE WRONG COFFEE FILTERS
I BOUGHT A YEAR AGO AND
FORGOT TO RETURN.

BOOKS I WON'T READ AGAIN,
BUT SOMEONE WILL! →

The last pile is a "moving on" pile for anything that makes you feel small or constricted or unbearably sad. (Ultimately, you may throw these things away or donate them, but they get a little send-off, a formal, cleansing recognition from you that they no longer serve you.) If they have sentimental value, or if dealing with them makes you squirmy and uncertain, you can have a friend store them until you're ready to part with them for good.

2. Once you've got your piles sorted, take everything that's left and make it pretty (or logical, or alphabetical, or color-coordinated).
3. Finally, the fun part: stand back, and gaze at your beautiful new space.

GETTING Organized Makes Room For BETTER BIGGER Messes

❐ DAY 16: UNPLUG

Every now and then, I take a digital hiatus. Most often, it's to go camping or hiking in places without wireless access. Those breaks have taught me a lot of things, but the single most important thing I've learned is that unplugging from the digital world creates space in the physical world.

I want to make it clear that I'm not opposed to social media. I love my Facebook community. I love how Twitter connects me to people and news all over the world, instantly. I'm inspired regularly by the things I see on Instagram, and yet . . .

Unplugging is powerful. There is a level of quiet that can only be reached when you firmly plant yourself in the 3-D world. It's a stillness that isn't really still at all. It's made of earth and sky and life bursting out all over the place. It's made of the connections that can only happen with actual voices, actual smiles, skin-to-skin contact, heart-to-heart hugs.

Truth be told, I'm an Internet junkie. I fill every lull in my day with information, commentary, and silliness from my online community. What I've noticed is that when the Internet isn't an option, I fill those lulls with books, walks, music, and art.

On a digital hiatus, I write more, draw more, adventure more. I talk to my neighbors, play with my dog, and plant things in the ground. I inhabit fully my 3-D life.

To be clear, I'm not even the slightest bit interested in living off the grid. I love my online community fiercely, but I do think that it's a good idea, every now and then, to step away from the virtual and into the physical.

Today, make a list of the things you might do on a digital hiatus. Imagine turning off your computer, your smart phone, and your television, and then fill your list with activities and adventures that don't require an electrical outlet. Once you have your list, schedule yourself a day off, and do one or more of the things on it.

Have fun!

THINGS TO DO ON A DIGITAL HIATUS

❐ DAY 17: MAKE A SONGS-TO-BELT LIST

I readily admit that there are things more pleasant than listening to me sing. Mowing the grass comes to mind. Grocery shopping. Visiting the dentist.

Even so, I love to sing, and I wonder if there is anybody who doesn't. Lack of talent and threat of embarrassment aside, who doesn't like to sing (and occasionally belt) their favorite songs?

Years ago I made a "Songs to Belt" CD for a friend (back before there were playlists). I don't know if she liked any of the songs, but I loved collecting them for her. It was fun because not every song I like is a song I love to belt, but some are irresistible. "Bohemian Rhapsody," anyone?

Today, make your "Songs to Belt" playlist and then sing it, baby, at the top of your lungs!

SONGS TO BELT

◻ DAY 18: BE UNAPOLOGETIC

A couple of years ago, I noticed how often I was apologizing. Reflexively. Because it was easier and certainly more expedient than an explanation. But it wasn't just that I used an apology to swiftly discharge a potentially tense encounter or soften a difficult message. I apologized for the weather, for traffic, for all kinds of things that were not only not my fault, but nobody's fault. I once apologized for being on vacation when someone was trying to reach me . . . and, honestly, I wasn't sorry at all.

The trouble with apologizing all the time is that it diminishes you. It's one of the many ways we make ourselves smaller so that others might feel bigger, and seriously, we need to stop that.

You are worthy, you are awesome, and you do not have to apologize for that.

I know I'm not the only compulsive apologizer.

It happens all the time-people apologizing for things they need not feel bad about. If you never do that, yay! Today will be easy for you. If you do, it might surprise you how engrained your urge to apologize has become.

But not today! Today, only say you're sorry if you truly owe someone an apology. Think about it first. Decide if it's real. (Hint: if you bump into someone accidentally, the right term is "Excuse me," not "I'm sorry.") Be discerning. Say sorry only when you really, truly are.

And then, after you've spent the day being big, brave, and unapologetic, you can come back here and color the cupcake I drew you on the next page. You deserve it!

☐ DAY 19: WRITE A SELF-LOVE MANTRA

Sometimes I can't believe the things I say to myself. I truly believe that if I talked to my friends the way I all too often talk to myself, I'd have no friends at all. I'm sure you wrestle with your own inner voice, the one who judges you constantly and always finds you lacking.

What I want you to do today is write yourself a self-love mantra, a positive phrase or affirmative statement that you say to yourself in a conscious effort to silence your inner critic.

Here's how I want you to do it. Imagine your dearest friend says to you . . .

"PLEASE WRITE ME A LOVE MANTRA, SOMETHING THAT WILL REMIND ME I'M WORTHY AND LOVED. I WANT YOU TO WRITE IT BECAUSE YOU REALLY SEE ME AND LOVE ME WITH CLEAR EYES. I'M GOING TO READ YOUR MANTRA TO MYSELF WHENEVER I'M FEELING INSIGNIFICANT AND UNSURE. IT'LL REMIND ME NOT TO GET CAUGHT UP IN THAT LITTLE INNER VOICE THAT SAYS I'M NOT GOOD (SMART, BIG, SAVVY, TALENTED) ENOUGH. IT'LL REMIND ME TO EMBRACE MY NATURALLY BADASS WAYS. IT'LL REMIND ME THAT NO MATTER HOW ALONE I FEEL...I'M NOT."

If your friend said that to you, you wouldn't hesitate, would you? You'd write her a kickass, take-no-prisoners love mantra to remind her daily how wonderful she is.

So today, write yourself a love mantra (or two, or three, or ten). Say all the things you need to hear when you're feeling doubtful and insecure. Write a mantra to inspire and empower you, a mantra that will remind you daily how wonderful (and smart, and loving, and fierce, and beautiful) you are.

If it feels right, ask someone you love to write a mantra for you, too. I did that. Five times. I have five beautiful, kickass love mantras that hang above my work table, and I read them every day.

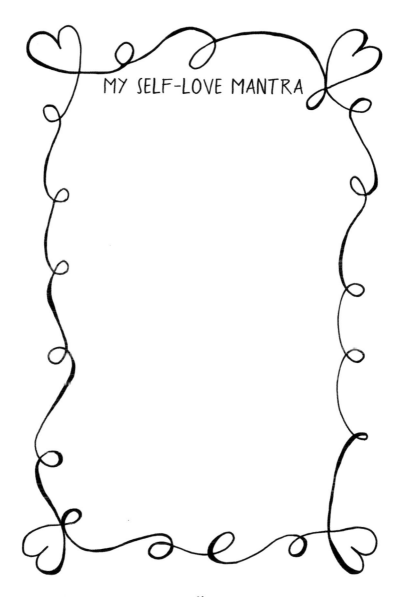

MY SELF-LOVE MANTRA

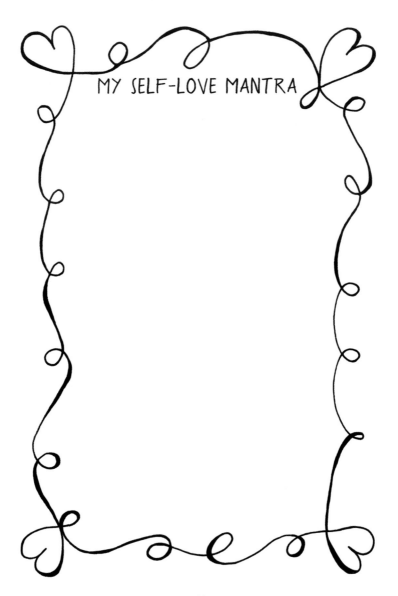

MY SELF-LOVE MANTRA

❏ DAY 20: WRITE YOUR PERSONAL MANIFESTO

I love manifestos. I love the certainty of them, the optimism of writing out your aspirations as *faits accomplis*, the boldness of life plans deeply rooted in personal values. They're mission statements with personality, business plans for the soul.

Today, begin crafting your personal manifesto. Think of it as equal parts value statement and call to action. Writing (or doodling, or drawing) a personal manifesto is a fun and creative way to get clear on who you are and what you want.

Dig deep. Put it all down: where you're going, how you're getting there, the beliefs and principles that guide you every step of the way. Here are some questions that might be helpful to think about . . .

1. What do I stand for?
2. What do I believe?
3. How do I want to live my life?
4. What impact do I want to have?
5. What makes me happy, fulfilled, hopeful?

Take your time. A personal manifesto is a big thing. It may take more than one day, and that's fine. Be imaginative and brave: this is you, as art.

If you need inspiration, here's mine. Plus, you can get more ideas by searching "manifesto" in Google Images. People are amazing.

BE HONEST Choose
BE BRAVE Love
BE EVOLUTIONARY
Blaze my own trail
wear comfortable shoes
Be curious Find beauty
Question the Status Quo • Be Curved • Make More Art
Doodle with Heart LEAP
Stand for something beautiful
BE Human & Kind

84

☐ DAY 21: LEAVE IT HERE

Worry, it seems, is a natural byproduct of life's ebb and flow. Worry, along with stress, overthinking, and second-guessing. We fret about things big and small, things we can change and things we can't, real things and things we only imagine in our fraught and spun-up state. We forget that every minute we spend worrying is a moment we haven't spent living because it's impossible to be fully present in your life and worried at the same time.

Worry takes you out of the current moment by hijacking your thoughts and splitting your attention. When you're worried, there is always the thing you're worried about, and then there's whatever is actually happening in your life right this minute . . . with, or without you.

By definition, you can't be fully engaged with your life if you're letting worry and stress have their way with you.

So today, I invite you to leave your worries here. Fill up these thought bubbles with whatever you're worried about right now. Your concerns might be as big as the health of the planet or as small as what to make for dinner tonight. Whatever your current worries are, write them here. (Use colored pens, and maybe some doodles because, you never know . . . perspective moves in mysterious ways.)

Once you've written your worries down, close this journal and head into your day. You can relax, knowing your worries are being safely stored here while you concentrate on experiencing your real, right-in-front-of-you, reach-out-and-dance-with-it life.

For all of today's moments, try to stay present and aware because, in the end, Oprah Winfrey is right when she says, "This very moment is the only one you know you have for sure."

☐ DAY 22: LEAVE LOVE LYING AROUND

If it's true that what you put out into the world comes back to you (and I believe with all my heart that it is), then why not put love out there? *Lots of it.* All over the place.

One thing I learned during my year of fearless love is that when you're feeling in need of a little TLC (as we all do sometimes), then "being the love you need" is amazingly effective. It feels good in that way that only giving love can, like sunbeams lighting you up from the inside.

So today, expand your heart. Leave love lying around for people to find. Here are a few suggestions to get you started:

WAYS TO LEAVE LOVE LYING AROUND

LEAVE ENCOURAGING NOTES IN SURPRISING PLACES, LIKE LIBRARY BOOKS AND SUBWAY SEATS.

WRITE LIPSTICK MESSAGES ON THE MIRROR.

POST LOVING TEAR-OFF POSTERS IN YOUR NEIGH-BORHOOD. (FOR INSPIRATION AND EVEN PDF PRINT-ABLES, GOOGLE "LOVING TEAR-OFF POSTERS.")

WRITE LOVE SONG LYRICS IN CHALK ON THE SIDEWALK.

TUCK A SILLY DRAWING INTO A LUNCH BOX.

DROP A THANK YOU NOTE IN THE MAILBOX FOR THE MAIL PERSON.

DECLARE YOUR LOVE IN POST-IT NOTES.

TUCK A FLOWER UNDER A WINDSHIELD WIPER.

SLIP A LOVE NOTE INTO A POCKET WHILE FOLDING THE LAUNDRY.

LEAVE CHOCOLATE ON SOMEONE'S PILLOW.

⌐ DAY 23: PRACTICE PLEASURE

In her wonderful e-book, *How to Change the World*, Lissa Rankin, MD outlines 15 attributes of the successful visionary. Number three on the list? Self-care. "Inspired visionaries fill themselves first so they can make the world a better place," she writes. "Although it's tempting to deplete ourselves in the process of serving the world, doing so serves no one."

Amen.

So how does Rankin suggest we fill ourselves first? One way is to "practice pleasure."

I love that phrase. The idea of having a pleasure practice makes me a little bit giddy. "Relish what feels good," Rankin writes, and the word "relish" delights me. It's like an invitation to joy.

You can't "relish" an activity unless you're fully present, fully engaged. Practicing pleasure isn't just about doing what you love; it's about surrendering to it. It's about doing what you do—creating, reading, hiking, writing, dancing, gardening, running, knitting, cooking, making friends, making art, making love—with everything you've got, savoring the experience, letting delight rearrange your insides.

Today, make pleasure your practice. Experiment with what lights you up inside, and feel your own radiance, your own undeniable bliss.

Then come back here and write all about it.

happy happy hap

_____

_____

_____

_____

_____

_____

_____

_____

_____

_____

_____

_____

☐ DAY 24: MAKE A *NOT*-TO-DO LIST

As you forge your path of tenacious self-love, the things you decide *not* to do are sometimes just as important as the things you decide to start or continue doing.

Today I want you to make a list of what you can stop doing in order to make room for all the cool stuff you want to do.

HOW I SPEND MY SPARE TIME

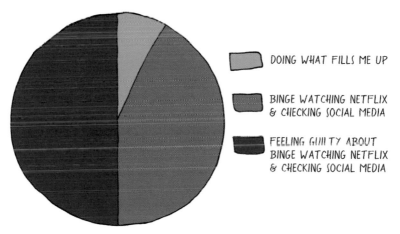

DOING WHAT FILLS ME UP

BINGE WATCHING NETFLIX & CHECKING SOCIAL MEDIA

FEELING GUILTY ABOUT BINGE WATCHING NETFLIX & CHECKING SOCIAL MEDIA

There are undoubtedly many, many ways to approach your not-to-do list. Here are three possibilities:

1. Create space in your life.

   To make more space, go after obvious time wasters, like surfing the Internet or taking 100 selfies in order to get just one that isn't embarrassing. (What, you don't do that?)

2. Make good health a priority.

   To get healthier, your not-to-do list might include unhealthy habits like eating sugar, going to bed late, and smoking cigars.

3. Become more productive.

   To get more productive, try this. Write a list of everything you need to do. Circle the five most important things. Everything else on your list becomes your not-to-do list. Instant prioritization!

As you make your list, avoid generalizations. Writing "I won't procrastinate," or "I won't put myself last" isn't specific enough to actually open up space in your day. "I won't check e-mail more than twice a day" is better. It's clear and actionable. The time you spend not going through your inbox can be spent doing something creative and soul-filling.

Here's my not-to-do list . . .

MY NOT-TO-DO LIST

I WON'T LEAVE FACEBOOK ON IN THE BACKGROUND
WHILE I WORK.

I WON'T SUBSCRIBE TO ANYTHING NEW WITHOUT
GETTING RID OF SOMETHING OLD.

I WON'T SAY YES TO PEOPLE WHO UNDERVALUE ME,
OR TO PROJECTS THAT FEEL MORE DRAINING THAN
EXCITING.

I WON'T LET PERFECT BE THE ENEMY OF DONE.

I WON'T LEAVE MY WORKOUT FOR THE END OF THE
DAY.

Use this page to write your not-to-do list.

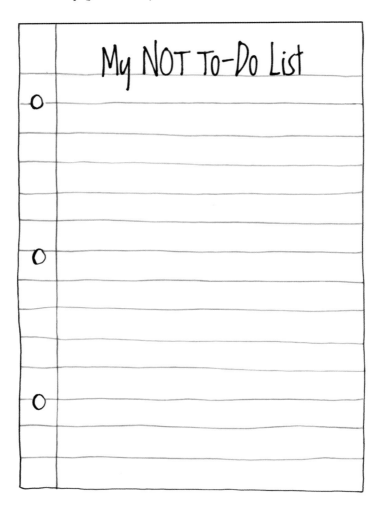

My NOT To-Do List

❐ DAY 25: DECIDE WHAT MATTERS

Once upon a time, I read a piece on the *New York Times* website in which Megan Stielstra told the story of her apartment building catching on fire. From the moment their neighbor pounded on their door, Stielstra and her husband had just a few minutes to consider what they would save.

I was particularly moved by the story because of something that had happened to me years before, a few months after my husband and I were married. While moving from one side of town to another, our U-Haul, loaded with all our belongings, was stolen. A few days later, the police recovered the van outside the city dump, empty.

It was strange to have the material part of our lives erased so completely and so suddenly. The loss was like nothing else I'd ever experienced-the bewildering bigness of it and also the weird sort of smallness. Of course the furniture, clothes, and dishes were all replaceable. Much harder to process were the journals and photo albums, the shoe box of keepsakes, the hand-written card from my uncle who died of Alzheimer's not long after sending it. None of these things would have held any interest to the thief. These were the priceless pieces of my life tossed away at the city dump, the things I might have rescued if I'd had the chance.

In Megan Stielstra's story, that chance was what fascinated me-those precious few minutes when she had to focus her racing mind and decide what had meaning in her life. I'd never experienced that. Again and again, I imagined the things I would grab if I had.

I asked my blog readers to tell me what they'd rescue, and their answers were so touching, sometimes surprising, often funny.

OUR LIVES &
WORK ARE
SAVED ON OUR
DEVICES

THE BOURBON
"TO TOAST
WATCHING ALL
OUR STUFF
BURN"

PACKED & READY
FOR EMERGENCY

CASH STASH
(CLEVERLY DISGUISED)

OUR
SECRETS

PICTURES OF
THE ONES WE
LOVE

OUR BELOVED
PETS

GLASSES, KEYS,
WALLET, SHARPIES
KLEENEX, CAPE

I think there's value in thinking about it, a sort of personal alchemy of considerations, both practical and emotional ... a little material mapping of your heart.

Take a few minutes now to imagine it yourself, then list (or doodle, or wax poetic) about the personally precious things you would rescue from a fire.

THINGS I'D RESCUE FROM THE FIRE

❏ DAY 26: TAKE A BREAK

Consciously, deliciously, take a break today and fill it however you want to. Here are some doodles to color in case you want to take your break right here, practicing the art of doing nothing.

SHOW 'em YOUR HeaRT.

☐ DAY 27: BE SURPRISING

It's so easy to find yourself on autopilot, your mind ticking through your to-do list as you run from place to place getting stuff done. Even very busy days tend to unfold in predictable ways: phone calls are made, appointments are kept, dinner is served, television is watched. We sleep before we do it all again.

Today, make a conscious effort to surprise yourself. Surprise other people. Do things that are unexpected. Do things you wouldn't ordinarily do. Go on a hike during your lunch break or read a book in the park. Buy yourself flowers. Study the sky. Invite someone to coffee. Blow a kiss. Bake a cake.

Today, be irreverent, silly, spontaneous, joyful. Wake up your world!

WAKE PEOPLE UP TODAY!

❏ DAY 28: DRAW A SELF-PORTRAIT

Don't worry, this isn't an artistic thing (necessarily); it's more of a "what do you want to capture about you and your life *right now*" thing. It doesn't matter if the portrait looks like you, or even if it looks like a person. Here are your instructions:

1) Let go of any notion that there is a right or wrong way to do this. Instead, be determined to dance with yourself here, to capture the you that maybe only you know.

2) Draw yourself lovingly. Even if your picture is about what scares or frustrates you, draw it as a friend would–with compassion, with tenderness.

Here's my self-portrait.

MY PENS

MY T-SHIRT LIFE PHILOSOPHY

MY SWEET, SPAZZY DOG

A PALM TREE TO SYMBOLIZE MY LOVE OF HOT WEATHER

YOUR TURN!

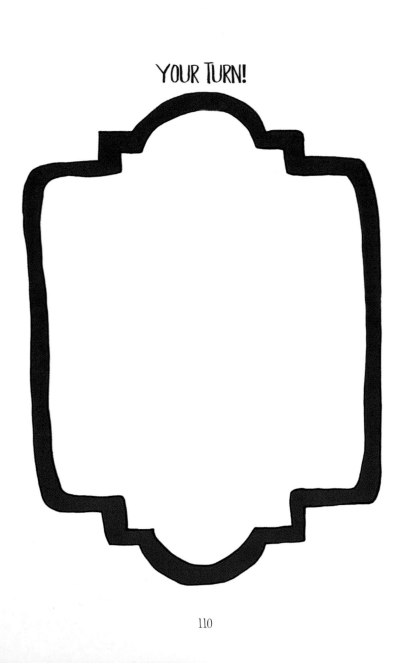

☐ DAY 29: WRITE YOURSELF A LOVE LETTER

It's Day 29. By now, I'm hoping you've begun to realize how capable of joy and badassery you are. Still, you might find writing yourself a love letter to be challenging. If so, don't worry! It's just a new skill you haven't had a chance to master. Pretend you're writing to your best friend if that helps, and then make a big deal out of yourself. Recognize your leaps; your moments of insight; your fortitude; your intuition; your kindness; your bravery; your big, beautiful, loving heart. You're an incredible, ever-changing being. Love your evolution.

DEAR INCREDIBLY EVOLUTIONARY,
INSIGHTFUL, IMAGINATIVE,
OPENHEARTED, ADVENTUROUS SELF:

YOU ARE BRAVER AND STRONGER
THAN ANYONE REALIZES, AND I LOVE YOU!
I LOVE YOU FOR TAKING THE TIME TO
LOVE YOURSELF, FOR REALIZING THAT ALL LOVE STARTS
WITH SELF-LOVE, AND THAT YOU ARE ABSOLUTELY
WORTHY OF YOUR OWN CARE AND ATTENTION.
I LOVE YOUR BEAUTIFUL, MESSY HEART,
AND I WILL NEVER
LET YOU DOWN.

Love, Me

I even made some colorable doodly stationery for you to use to write on.

❏ DAY 30: DESIGN A BOOK COVER FOR YOUR LIFE STORY

Imagine the title of your life story. (Here's what I imagined for mine.)

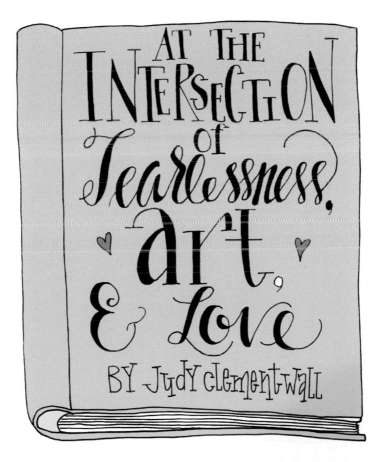

AT THE INTERSECTION of fearlessness, art, & love

BY Judy Clement-Wall

Your life story is the one you're writing every single day, from scratch, armed with nothing but your wits, your fortitude, and your big curious heart. Make no mistake about it, it is *your* story.

Believe in it. *Own it.* Love it fiercely. And don't let anyone else try to write it for you.

WHAT NOW?

First of all, congratulations, you did it! Take a minute to bask in your accomplishment. In a world of cynics, where snark and sarcasm hold sway over heart and soul, choosing love is an act of courage, and choosing to love yourself may be the most courageous act of all.

I believe it's also one of the most generous things you can do for yourself and for the world. There is no better gift you can give to the world than to bring into each day your best, most confident, most fully realized self-the person you become when you shower yourself with love.

I hope you'll keep your self love practice going. One way to do that is to take your favorite pages from this journal and make them into their own 30-day challenges. Try 30 days of gratitude, 30 days of being wildly creative, or 30 days of practicing pleasure.

Whatever you do, don't let it end here. You are inarguably *AWE-SOME*. Don't be afraid to let that show.

You're a self-love hero!

ABOUT THE AUTHOR

JUDY CLEMENT WALL is a writer/illustrator whose work has been published in numerous literary journals and on websites such as the *Huffington Post, Mind Body Green,* and *The Good Men Project.* She is an illustrator for HCI Book's popular *Inkspirations* coloring book series, and her whimsical artwork can be found on everything from greeting cards to lampshades to wine labels. Her mission as an artist is to inspire fearless love, soulful evolution, and wild creativity as a way of life. She lives in the San Francisco Bay Area and online at *judyclementwall.com.*